PRECI

LASTING HILLS

ISOBEL KUHN

Precious Things
of the
Lasting Hills

"Blessed of the Lord be his land, . . . for
the precious things of the lasting hills."
Deut. 33. 13, 15

OMF BOOKS

© OVERSEAS MISSIONARY FELLOWSHIP

First published	..	..	*August 1938*
	with three reprints		
Revised edition	..	..	*July 1950*
Reprinted with revisions		..	*May 1963*
Eight reprints	..	..	*1963–1977*
Reprinted ..	..	..	*September 1979*

ISBN 0 85363 044 5

Made in Great Britain
Published by the Overseas Missionary Fellowship
Belmont, The Vine, Sevenoaks, Kent, TN13 3TZ
and printed by Stanley L. Hunt (Printers) Ltd.
Rushden, Northants

CONTENTS

PUBLISHER'S NOTE

THIS little book, Isobel Kuhn's first, was written when, as a young missionary, she went with her husband and baby daughter to live among the Lisu tribespeople in south-west China. This is a simple recital of experiences recorded during the most impressionable period of a missionary's life—the first term of service.

The qualities that have endeared the author of *By Searching* to so many who never met her personally are revealed here in a completely unself-conscious way.

CHAPTER ONE

EXCALIBUR

"THE operation is to be to-morrow, at ten o'clock in the morning. They've got the next room all ready, scrubbed and sterilized, and they've even got me scrubbed and sterilized too!" My husband's face smiled bravely from his pillow and he indicated a bandaged place on his side where Doctor was to cut the next day. It was cosy in the little lamp-lit room. Outside dark had fallen, and the fierce mountain wind for which Tali is famous would come whirling down the steep ravines of the hills west of us and hurl itself against our native house and make it shiver. We were talking quietly together when steps bounded up the staircase, the door was quickly opened and our young doctor entered. Closing the door and leaning against it, he inwardly gripped his excitement so that it would not appear in his voice, but his tell-tale eyes were glowing with news.

"A strange thing has happened, and I've come for your advice and prayers. Ernest and Ruth (our host and hostess) went out for a walk a while ago, and as they returned several soldiers were walking just in front of them, but as they got up to our compound, one of the soldiers suddenly cried out, clutched his stomach, doubled up, and fell down *right at our doorway*! Ernest had him carried in and called me. It is obviously a case of perforated gastric; if he is not operated on he will be dead in a few hours. I am wondering if this is God's answer to our prayers that we might get a door into the barracks. Shall I operate?" and his face glowed with excitement (he is a born surgeon and had never done a gastric ulcer all by himself before!) as he came forward gently, sat down by the bed, and waited for our verdict.

A mile to the north of us was a big soldiers' barracks, and at this time some thousands of men were bivouacked there. In his daily walks, the doctor had often passed by their gates, and the burden of these who might any time soon be sent to their death, without Christ and without hope, had come upon him. So in the days while we were waiting for my husband to gather together enough strength to meet his operation, we at Tali had been praying daily that God would revive the work in our midst and that He would open to us a door into those barracks.

"Doesn't it seem strange," continued Doctor, still thrilled, "that this should happen at precisely this time, when the operating room is all sterilized and everything set for such an event? Your operation can easily wait over another day. What do you think?"

There was much involved; a precarious operation on a strange soldier. What would the military say? We thought it best to call the family to prayer, then, as we knelt around the bed, we asked our Father to tell us: was this from Him? We cast out two fleeces: one was if the military authorities gave an unconditional consent; the other, if after an hour or so we were *all* united in feeling we should go forward. By the time specified both fleeces answered, "Yes. Operate."

My, what a bustle ensued! Nurse (she is especially well qualified and experienced—indeed, Doctor praised her and called her "House-Surgeon") flew like a white bird up and down stairs and along the narrow corridors of that old Chinese house, and in a little time the home-made theatre was all in its white drapery and everything in place. We were all pressed into service! One was in charge of the boiling water supply: Ruth (who is also a nurse) gave the anaesthetic, assisted by her husband, who was properly covered up in one of her professional aprons, and who also had instructions to hold down the patient if he proved "naughty"! I had charge of the guests, for, of course, the medical officers from the Army were not going to miss the opportunity to see a white man's skill. And the rumour having got abroad that the foreign doctor was going to operate, other officers (and even a wife!) appeared on the scene. But as that was really much too many, my husband who was in bed next door, asked them into his room, where they could hear, if not see.

A gastric ulcer operation in a private house in *inland* China, with only two experienced helpers! A pressure lamp was rented and hung over the wooden "operating" table; as all the necessary implements were not in Doctor's possession he and Nurse had improvised substitutes, among them two table forks whose handles they curved back into the desired shape. Remembering this, we had to laugh when later on the military medicals solemnly assured us that they could have done these things too if only they had had the proper instruments! Soldier Jo's stomach had to be made clean on the outside, of course, and we will not soon forget Nurse's efforts on that long-unwashed, as she prepared him with a scrubbing brush! Happy confidence filled the atmosphere and just before Jo went under chloroform, prayer was made for him in Chinese. It was all over in an hour. Then prayer was made again, asking God's blessing and seal on the work done, and that not only his life be saved, but his soul as well. An improvised stretcher was made and the unconscious patient carried down to the room beneath John's, which had to do for hospital ward for some weeks thereafter.

And now our opportunity had come. Not only were we all freely invited to work in the barracks, but soldiers came eagerly to us in our compound. Of course, every day there were two who came especially to attend to Soldier Jo, and as these were changed often we had many chances to present the Lord Jesus. And Jo himself? He recovered perfectly. At first he was a bit obstreperous. I can still feel the angry kick of his foot as he refused to let me take off his shoes, which he was wearing in bed! And I can still hear the angry howl with which the soldier attendant leaped upon him and whipped them off regardless! That howl and rough action showed that discipline, not love, is the order of the Army.

But it was "love" that tended Jo day and night in the form of our dear Nurse, to whom nothing was too much bother, and who slipped in a testimony for the Lord Jesus whenever she could. Every missionary should come to the field with two weapons for his warfare against heathenism. In his left hand he should wield the weapon of Prayer, and in his right the Sword of the Spirit, which is the Word of God; the one to be used in battling with the unseen principalities and powers, the other for the visible flesh and blood, and the barriers which it throws up against him and his message. These weapons must always be of one certain make—no other is efficient. That of Prayer is bedded in a hilt of the metal of faith and is engraved all over with these words, "Not my will but Thine be done"; for effectual prayer must spring out of faith and out of a whole-hearted consecration that will say "Yes, Lord" at any moment, and in reply to any call from Him.

The right-hand weapon, used in visible warfare is a delicate blade, so beautiful and precious in workmanship that it reminds me of that famous and exquisite sword, the Excalibur of Arthur. As to the blade itself, there is only one which can "pierce to the dividing asunder of soul and spirit" (the Holy Writ). But Excalibur had something more than its blade; it was rich

> With jewels, elfin Urim, on the hilt,
> Bewildering heart and eye—the blade so bright
> That men are blinded by it. . . .

It was that shine of bewildering glory which, in battle, subdued men's hearts before it ever touched their bodies. So it is with the sword-of-the-right-hand. For every "Yes, Lord" engraved upon the left-hand weapon there appears a jewel of *love* upon the hilt of the right-hand blade, a jewel of deep passion for Christ, until the Sword of the Spirit is one dazzling glory of constraining love. It is this sheen of love that breaks down barriers of race, religious prejudices, everything, and leaves the heathen heart open for the naked blade to enter—the convicting work of the Spirit of God. I have seen it so often: dull, care-worn "closed" faces, when they meet that shining touch of one of Christ's lovers of souls, suddenly open up with a great wistfulness, a shyly dawning light of welcome.

One evening, after a long and hard day's work, the doctor went in to see Jo, who was then up and convalescing. I went in also to see if any help was needed. The little room was dark, except for the glow of a coal fire in an iron bowl the Chinese call a "fire-basin". Soldier Jo was seated there brewing some tea for himself, and for a young soldier lad who was his attendant that night. At our entrance the latter got up immediately and insisted that the doctor take his chair, and as he did so, the soldier laddie sat down at his feet. Doctor is tall and big-framed, but he is not physically strong, and he was very tired that evening.

Soldier Jo yielded his chair to me and then squatted in front, and we began to talk, with the firelight throwing its red glow over the four of us. I asked Jo if by now he had taken the Lord Jesus into his heart as Saviour, and he said yes, but so weakly that it led to conversation on that dear Redeemer and His death for us upon the Cross. Jo's eyes were riveted in attention on my face, but I was conscious also of a sweet drama going on at the left. The doctor was using Excalibur; he had slipped his arm around the soldier lad's shoulders, and the latter had turned to him a look of amazement which gradually shaded off into wonder and then into wistfulness. The big foreign doctor so to condescend to him, a mere common cipher of a Chinese soldier? To him those in high places had only shown harshness and contempt, but his boy heart was hungry, and here was one to whom his highest officer .bowed respectfully actually putting an arm around his shoulders! He was too thrilled to listen to what the white woman was saying, but with the wonder of this new friend glowing in his face, he shyly reached out and touched the doctor's knee. Finding he was not repulsed, he snuggled up and whispered, "How old are you?"

"Twenty-six" came from the shadows into which the doctor had disappeared as he leaned back wearily in his chair.

"Shut up and listen!" growled Jo, who was simply drinking in "that sweet story of old" and who had been distracted for a moment by the whisper. A touch from Doctor urging silence brought Laddie to attention, and he found himself listening to an account of another Life, a life so selfless, so loving, that instinctively the boy felt it must be linked up closely with that tender pressure around his shoulders, and he became enthralled. As the story went on approaching that most sacred spot of Calvary, with all its wonderful, beautiful detail, the earnest gaze of Soldier Jo, the wistful boy-eyes of Laddie, the red firelight and dusky shadows seemed to disappear and we all stood upon a faraway hill with its three crosses; we shivered as the noonday sun turned to black darkness, we trembled as the earth shook beneath our feet, and we thrilled as we heard the cry of "Finished!" ascend

in triumph up through the sorrowing heavens to the throne of
God. Then the peace of that Easter morning stole in upon us, and
the heart-bursting joy of the risen Lord's tender assurance, "Be
not afraid; it is I!" made us draw in our breath. As the words
ended a solemn silence filled the shadowy fire-lit room. There
was One standing there, holding out His nail-scarred hands to
two heathen hearts and all thoughts were upon Him. Forgotten
in the radiance of this greater light was the human love which
had first revealed Him to Laddie's amazed gaze, and now his
eyes were looking out in wistful hunger into the shadow-filled
room.

"Little Brother, won't you take Him as your own Saviour, to-
night?"

The words startled Laddie into attention.

"But I can't read!" he said, as if standing on the outside of a
barred gate.

"You don't need to," came in Doctor's voice from the dark
shadows. "He is a *Person*. All you need to do is to *know* Him, and
receive Him."

"Little Brother, do you know the doctor?"

"Yes," he replied, turning to gaze at his new friend with a
smile of shy love.

"But you say you cannot read. How can you know the doctor?
Don't you see that taking Christ as Saviour is just the same as
taking a new friend into your heart? Only this Friend must
become Master. The more time you spend with Him, the better
you know Him. It is not a question of reading, but *of getting to
know Him*, and then obeying His voice. When we talk to Him we
call it praying. Won't you talk to Him now and ask Him to
come into your life and save you from sin as your Saviour and
Lord?"

The young face considered it thoughtfully a moment, and
then looked up and smiled "Yes."

So there in the firelight, Laddie, guided by the missionaries,
talked to Him of Calvary and asked Him to "forgive, come in
and rule." Oh, the joy of the quiet that followed that prayer!
Where are they now, those two common soldiers of China who
faced Christ that night—Jo of earnest gaze and Laddie of the

wistful eyes? About two years later a missionary in another city sent me word that Laddie was stationed there and coming to church and wished to send us word that he was still a Christian. The Friend they invited in that evening says He will never forsake those who trust Him. "He never yet put out a dim candle that was lighted at the Sun of Righteousness." Dim candles are they both, illiterate, common soldiers ordered from place to place, with no settled abode, few Christian friends to help and teach them. We who love them can only commit them to our faithful Master and pray for them.

> And wherever they may bide,
> Lead them home at eventide.

As I went upstairs I wondered just how genuine Laddie's profession had been. So soon does Satan send Doubt to nip at the heels of Faith. Had he really understood? Had he said "Yes" just to please us? Just to be nice? Thus yelped the heel-nipper.

Our last Sunday at Tali (for we were under orders to move into Lisuland as soon as we could travel) my husband had been asked to preach at the big noon service. The men's side of the church was thronged with soldiers, so at the end my husband gave the invitation, asking for raised hands from those who would take, or had during the last few weeks taken, Christ as Saviour. A hand went up. I leaned forward eagerly to see who it was that had the courage to proclaim himself a Christian in front of so many fellow soldiers. I gave one look, then sank back in my pew crying in my heart, "Oh, thank God. It's Laddie." For so it was; his face, looking up at the man in the pulpit, was simple and sincere, and his hand, raised awkwardly, was visible to all. In a minute or so Soldier Jo's hand went up too (that day he looked pale and weak, not so earnest as Laddie) and then a hand here and there, each one being received with much gaping and nudging of elbows by the heathen Army men.

Then from my husband, "Will all of you that mean it come out from your seats to the front?"

My heart failed me. "Isn't that asking too much?" But no! Out walked eleven soldiers and lined up in front of the pulpit.

"Now all of you get down on your knees right here, and pray to Christ to forgive you your sins."

Down on the stone flags went eleven pairs of knees; then a blue shadow slipped down the aisle, went in and knelt with them. It was Doctor. John was down among them too by this time, and together they helped each of those men to pray for salvation, though I must admit that one or two looked as if courage were reaching for his hat to flee! But they all stuck to their places, and stayed until their names were registered and they were dismissed.

By this time I was on the organ stool facing the grey uniforms; and as they stood in line before breaking up, it so happened that Laddie and another soldier boy whom I had also pointed to the Lord in the weeks just passed, were standing together at the end of the row nearest the organ. As the line was dismissed and they turned to go, each boy (unknown to the other) bent his head and shot a quick smile at the one on the organ seat. Both smiles said the same thing: "I knew you'd be glad to know *I meant it!*"

"Will there be any stars in my crown?" says an old hymn. Who would care for stars when they might have such warm human smiles lined up in heaven awaiting them! "Ye are my joy and crown of rejoicing," said Paul.

> O teach me what it meaneth—
>   That Cross uplifted high,
> With One—the Man of Sorrows—
>   Condemned to bleed and die!
> O teach me what it cost Thee
>   To make a sinner whole
> And teach me, Saviour, teach me
>   The value of a soul!

One other scene comes up before me, and I may not but tell it. It was a case that Excalibur lost, though through no fault of its own; but one cannot forget the patient, for she left a scar upon the heart.

One morning at breakfast we were summoned to two cases at the same time, each of which was an attempted suicide through swallowing opium. (I usually went with the doctor as interpreter, for his Chinese was still in the early stages.) The first case was a girl of sixteen, and it took all Doctor's skill to bring her back, for she was far gone, but God purposed to save her life and she was restored.

As we left that house the second man, a poorly dressed fellow, was still waiting for us and said, "Now you must come to my place! There's a woman there who swallowed opium an hour or so ago," and as we went he proceeded with his story. "She is a poor tribeswoman who has had some trouble with her relatives-in-law and ran away from them. She came to our place late last night, and asked for lodging; she deceived us" (the man was bitter with anger) "and did not tell us she meant to commit suicide in our house; she just asked for a place to sleep. And then this morning my wife caught her swallowing the opium. It isn't fair. We are poor people and have no money for her coffin." In this part of China, if a stranger dies under your roof, you are responsible for his burial. The man was too filled with wrath to have any pity for a broken-hearted woman.

For broken-hearted she was. I never found out the details of her sorrow, but as she was married it was probably a cruel and hard mother-in-law. Our hapless patient seemed to be nearly thirty years of age and showed she was of the peasant class. She was easy to restore, but took the medicine unwillingly. (Her death was caused by re-swallowing some more opium secretly, later on in the same day, after we all thought she had been saved.) It was such a blank young face—blank and dull with despair, a face from which hope had fled. As we looked at that desolate hopelessness, as we saw the timid way in which she tried to refuse life-restoratives (timid because she evidently thought she'd be beaten or rough-handled if she did not take the medicine), we wondered how we could ever strike through that dead despair in order to challenge her consciousness to listen to what we had to say. Her mind was quite clear, but her heart was broken, and "life" had died within her. To talk to her was like talking into a telephone when the other party has hung up their receiver. We wanted to reach *her*, not just her physical ears. How stab that "her" alive again, alive enough to listen to what we had to say? Only Excalibur could pierce through such a barrier, so we used the most amazing words that such a one could ever have heard.

We said, "Sister, there is One who *loves* you, called Jesus."

Such a blow was sufficient, and for a moment we thought we had her, for the soul of her leaped up into her eyes with one great appeal, and then Reality (as she had known it) gripped it dead, and the blankness closed over it and she murmured wearily. "*Puh ai. Puh ai*" (literally "No love. No love," meaning "No, He doesn't. It's not so").

Reality that had only known a loveless past and could only look upon a loveless future had told her we were creating this big lie to deceive her back into life, and so she shook her head and in a tired voice said, "No love. No love." We left her sitting there, restored in body, but still dead in her heart. We meant to return to her soon, but later learned she had tricked us all and now lay dead in body too.

But let her words, symbolic of millions of her fellow sisters, haunt your heart as they have haunted mine. "No love. No love." *That is why she died*. She couldn't go on living without it, and she had ceased to hope there was such a thing for her. Lucky Laddie to have learned it before hope was dead.

But *is* there such a thing for a woman? "God so loved the *world* that he gave his only begotten Son, that whosoever believeth in him *should not perish* but have everlasting life." Do you know that rich love of God which is poured out upon His redeemed ones in a measure too great to receive? What do you do with your "overflow"? Do your neighbours share it? Is your Excalibur shining with it? Or rusty because it is never used? Do you open your heart to the aches and wounds of this old world, or do you quickly close it lest you be made uncomfortable with such distressing news? "Who shall separate us from the love of Christ?" Have you ever laid your head on that dear pillow? But there are those who *are* separated from it, by *ignorance of it*. Will you let the overflow of His love to you reach them?

CHAPTER TWO

THE SECOND MILE

To go the second mile means to do always your duty, and a
great deal more than your duty, in the spirit of loving devotion
that does not even know it has done its duty.—

Oswald Chambers.

LIFE has taught me some lessons. One of these is that it is often
the *extra effort* which finally swings the tussle into victory.
This is thrillingly illustrated in that grand description of a football
game, "Varsity *versus* McGill" (R. Connor's *The Prospector*).
Both teams are locked in a close scrimmage which is tiring the
men with advance to neither side. On the sideline is Black, the
captain of a famous team some years back, and his matured
experience tells him what is needed.

"For a few moments both teams hang in the balance, neither
giving an inch, when old Black, yelling and waving wildly,
attracts the attention of Bate" (full-back).

" 'Go in!' he cried. 'Go in!' and Bate, coming up with a rush,
throws himself behind the scrum.

"His weight turns the scale. Slowly at first, but gaining
momentum every inch the mass yields, sways, and begins to
move. The McGill men, shoving, hacking, scragging, fighting
fiercely, finally dropping on their knees, strive to check that
relentless advance. It is in vain. Their hour has come."

So it has been on the mission field very often. A regular day's
work has brought no results, but an extra hour added, in spite of
fatigue and discouragement, has often proved to be "Bate"—he
swung the scale.

My husband had had his operation in the interior of China so
as to enable us to answer the urgent need of a missionary couple
to take over a centre in a certain part of Lisuland. The way there
was difficult. We had to leave civilization as the Chinese know it,
and plunge into a great mountain fastness, making our road up
and over hills, through precipitous ravines, until, after a day and

a half, we came to the first of the twin rivers which chew abysmal canyons out of that broad mountain range. Up the narrow valley of the first river we went, and the third day's travel brought us to a town called in Chinese "Old City". The next day was Sunday, so we decided to spend that day in prayer and fasting—meet preparations for the beginning of a new and tremendous task.

Sunday broke into that little valley sunny and warm, so after feeding small three-year-old daughter Kathryn, we set out to find a place where we could be "private"—an impossibility in a crowded inn, and indeed a hopeless task, anyway, as we were to learn. Outside of the town was a small hillside leading down to the river, and we settled on its grassy brow with mutual congratulations. Plenty of plants and rocks to invite the curiosity of small Kathryn, fresh air and quiet for us bigger ones.

But alas and alack! we had settled down but a few minutes when around the side of a rock appears the interested countenance of a young cowherd. We groaned inwardly, knowing full well that Solitude had spread her wings and was waving us a fond goodbye! Sure enough. He disappeared for a short while and then reappeared *multiplied*. But there was absolutely nowhere else to go on that narrow shore, so we continued to have our Bible reading and prayers encircled by a line of smiling, whispering villagers, who thought it a great entertainment to see two white people sitting or kneeling on the ground in the open air, with their eyes closed and their lips moving, sometimes emitting strange sounds in a foreign tongue. Of course, "prayer" to the heathen is only uttered before an idol in a temple or the family ancestral tablet, etc. Converts have to be taught that God can hear them anywhere, at any time.

As one relay disappeared and another came to take its place, John would patiently explain to them what we were doing, and preach a little, and really we had a very nice time. One has to learn in China to forget one's surroundings and experience the truth of the beautiful Dohnavur poem:

> There is a viewless, cloistered room.
>   As high as heaven, as fair as day,
> Where, though my feet may join the throng,
>   My soul can enter in, and pray.

One hearkening even, cannot know
　　When I have crossed the threshold o'er,
For He alone who hears my prayer
　　Has heard the shutting of the door.

So "the door was shut" although our constant audience did not know it, and God blessed us with a message to our hearts which truly proved to be His preparation for what lay ahead.

About three o'clock we decided Kathryn should have something more to eat, so started back to the inn. But right next door to this "hotel" there was a prominent townsman holding a marriage feast for his son. Privacy is a thing which is wholly unattractive to the Sons of Sinim. So when they have a feast and their house cannot contain the guests, they proudly publish its narrowness by placing extra tables in the street.[1] The fact that the pigs and chickens and dogs grunt and cackle and bark around one's feet is of no significance, for they do so in the houses also. The lean and hungry look of the rest of the world who stand around watching merely acts as an appetizer, and so this jovial father had spread his hospitality at least two-thirds across the main thoroughfare of the town. They were just about to sit down and eat when we appeared on the scene, and immediately the townsman calls to us to come and join them; and indeed was so pressing and apparently sincere that we felt we had better accept. We were placed at the table of honour (the one in the middle of the street!) with the most important of the men guests, and so there was a splendid opportunity to tell of the Bread of Life, which God so generously offered to all men.

The meal over, Chinese women took hold of Small Girlie and me, and for the rest of the day we were going from house to house, explaining ourselves and our message to our varied audiences, and always keeping an eagle eye on what was said and done to precious little daughter. I never learned the filth of a heathen mind until I had a baby and discovered what the Chinese say to little ones. Need I explain that after hours of such strain I was very weary? And when darkness fell, and Kathryn had been washed and put into her bed, I decided to retire myself.

[1] This, of course, is small town life in a frontier province. I know little of life in the big cities of modern China.

It was a typical inn. We had, as usual, asked if we might sleep upstairs in rooms ordinarily less frequented and therefore a trifle cleaner, and had added that we preferred if other travellers did not sleep in the same room with us. Our request was courteously heeded and two upstairs rooms vacated for us; the outer room had no door to it, but there was a place for my camp-bed; the inner room necessitated sleeping on a Chinese bed, so my husband had taken that for himself, and Kathryn was placed there also. This left me to myself in the outer room without a door! So I undressed in the dark, lit my candle, got into bed and began having evening devotions there. I had just finished and blown out the candle when women's voices downstairs were heard addressing the innkeeper. "*Laopan! Laopan!* Where is the foreign woman?" I snuggled down under the bedclothes and comforted my conscience. "They are probably only more of the curious women guests. They probably wouldn't believe if I did get up and go to them; and, anyway, I'm too tired to preach any more to-day."

But the voices were loud and insistent. "Oh, she's upstairs, is she? Oh, I say! Lady! Lady! We've come to visit you." Silence in the upper region.

"*Laopan*, she does not answer. Is she really up there? It is all dark upstairs. Oh, she's really there, is she? Let's go up, anyhow" —followed by sniggers and Chinese bound feet pounding laboriously up the rickety wooden steps.

"*Ai-ya!* It's dark. Watch your step there! Wonder where she is. This way! I can feel with my feet. Take my hand. Yes, this is her room. Wonder where she . . . Oh! . . . what is it? Oh, it scared me, but it's only her table. No, I can't see anything, but I'm feeling round. Eh, what's this? A book! She must be here— here's her Holy Book. And here's something else. . . . What is it? Oh, her candle! What a find. Anybody got a match? Oh, here are *her* matches!" All this going on a few feet from my head, and I was lying there trying to keep down the giggles and (by this time) deliberately resolving to wait and see just how far they would go.

A scratch, a flame, and my candle was lit; its pure little light bringing into view the face of a Chinese married woman, a strong but not very intelligent face; behind her were some young girls of the student class, and, not seeing me, they all bent over the candle, then lifted it up and began to search the part of the room at the foot of my bed.

"Why! Here's something! Oh! It's a bed!" following it up until they discovered the occupant.

Bending down, the woman held the candle right close to my face and made the brilliant remark, "Why here she is!" Then there was no need to play any longer. Sitting up in bed with a laugh, I said, "Sure enough. Here she is!" Then, pulling my face into as dignified an expression as I could muster, I said mischievously, "Good evening, ladies. Won't you have a seat?"

Somewhat abashed at such courtesy, they fell back a bit and remarked they preferred to stand (which was very wise, as there were no seats!) and they could not stay long in any case. Not wishing to offend them, I stopped my teasing and said, "I have gone to bed, as you see, and cannot very well get up and take care of you; but if you like to talk to me here, I will be glad to answer your questions."

This put them at their ease and talk flowed freely. "Oh, don't think of getting up; we just want you to preach to us. Oh! So you wear clothes when you go to bed!" (examining them). "And you take your hair down at night! Does it take long to comb in the morning?" We women are the same the world over; but after a while they were satisfied they had seen all there was of interest, and the missionary quietly began:

"We foreigners have not come to your honourable country just to have a nice place to live. Our own home is quite comfortable."

"Oh, *is* it?" says the Uneducated One.

"Why surely," pipes up Miss Student, with a secret nudge for such ignorance. "Don't you know that America is the land of money?"

"Yes," goes on the missionary, "we left home, not because we were glad to get away from it, but because we love your honourable people and have a precious message to bring to them from the Creator of Heaven and earth. We do not worship Heaven and earth as you do, because they are inanimate objects.

We worship the One who made this world and all that is in it.

"That Maker is God. But just to know His name is not sufficient either, for none of us may come to Him as we are. We are not even able to pray to Him. Do you know why? Because He is separated from us by the fact that He is holy and we are sinful. God is absolutely pure, and therefore He may not come into contact with anything that is impure—or He would be no longer pure. So if you or I tried to come into His presence just as we are we would be consumed, just like a piece of paper if it approached my candle here. Our Holy Book says, 'God is a consuming fire,' and that means that everything impure or sinful would perish if it tried to come near Him. So you and I and the other people on this earth are in this hopeless condition. Because *some day* we must each of us reckon with our Creator as to the deeds done in the body. At that time, if our sins are still upon us, we will be cast out from God's presence into everlasting punishment—into hell. Every Chinese knows what hell is, does she not?

"Now, the precious Message which we have brought to you is just this: that God is *not only* 'a consuming fire,' but He is also compassionate love. And, because He loves you and me and all mankind, God found a way by which your and my sin may be forgiven us, and by which His own holiness may be given to us, thus allowing us to come to Him now in prayer and, in the future, to Heaven, the place where He abides. Is that not Good News?

"And now the important thing is that we learn what is the Way by which we may get rid of our sins. It was thus: God sent Jesus, His Son, to pay the penalty of your sins and mine. Now, God's holy law says, 'The soul that sinneth, it shall die,' so either you and I have to die for our sins or we must find a mediator who will do it for us. Jesus became that mediator and died for your and my sins."

Then followed a brief description of the Cross—for the Chinese know no such way of taking life—and, of course, the beautiful story of the Resurrection, the proof of His divinity and our redemption.

Some of you have asked how the missionary presents his

message to those who have never heard before. Therefore the above has been written to show you one way. It is really not difficult with those whose minds have been trained to think a little, as these young girls had.

When I finished, the little room was quiet, its darkness broken only by the small circle of candlelight and the thoughtful young faces, whose outward eye for once was blinded by the glory that had burst upon their inward gaze. Gently, I pushed the personal application: "This Gospel is true. God's Spirit is witnessing now in your own hearts that I have spoken the truth, but it is necessary that you each personally accept the payment of your debt to God, otherwise you must pay it yourself. Make your decision now."

"But Teaching-Mother, you are leaving here on the morrow. How can we know how to go on with this doctrine?"

"Well, little sister, you can read; and all this I have been telling you has been plainly written down in God's own book. I have no Chinese New Testaments here, but if you will give me your names and addresses, I will order a copy to be sent to each of you and you can read God's Way and God's Will for yourself. Will you accept Him now, if I do that?"

And three of them did. We had prayer together, I teaching them how He may be addressed, etc. Then their names were written down on a scrap of paper and given to me. Some months later, one of those New Testaments was returned to me through the mail; evidently a displeased parent had refused to allow the retention of the foreign book, but the other two must be with their owners—buried seed in a lonely little mountain town. I never saw any of them again.

After they had left and the diminished candle was again blown out, through the open window the silhouette of the mountains, crowned by stars—"the forget-me-nots of the angels"—looked in upon me, a look of quiet rebuke: "You were unwilling to go the second mile to-night, and yet of all your day it alone was bringing you fruit. Why aren't you steadfast like we are?"

Then the missionary, made of dust as they, but so much less faithful, bowed her head and asked forgiveness of Him who had died, that He might be able to grant it.

CHAPTER THREE

"MYRRH"

THE next morning we continued on our journey up the narrow valley to the night's resting-place, at the foot of one of the highest mountains I have ever climbed. And again in the early morning we started, up and up in a steep ascent that was seldom relieved by a curve, up past foliage that seemed to grow in belts, a pine-tree belt, a bamboo belt, and then near the great top the trees were entangled with long parasitical growths, hanging mosses and creepers. Crossing the top was a matter of a few yards, and there before us lay a grand panorama of peaks and crests and dark, shadowy lines which indicated abysmal canyons between them. "See those far distant summits? There's Lisuland!" said my husband.

Lisuland. At the far western edge of China there is a great mountain fastness, probably the petering off of the Tibetan plateau, but noble "peterings" they are—peaks of ten, twelve and fourteen thousand feet high. Through this huge chaotic pile, the twin rivers, rising in Tibet, cut parallel canyons many miles in length; and on the precipitous banks of these mighty gorges live human beings—the aboriginal tribespeople, driven into this back of beyond by the stronger, civilized Chinese.

One of these tribes is the Lisu. Far down in the south, the Flowery Lisu had heard and received the Gospel of salvation and in 1929 they sent four of their number up into the wilder northern reaches of the canyon to evangelize the Black Lisu. The work prospered, and by 1934 there were two churches, six days' journey apart, and only one missionary couple to care for them.

"My sheep wandered through all the mountains and upon every high hill . . . and none did search or seek after them" (Ezek. xxxiv. 6). The Lord had touched our hearts to offer to come in and care for the Oak Flat church, so that our dear senior missionaries might minister to the northern church. But preparation for such a task required thought. Imagine moving into a spot so isolated that the nearest source of supplies is six day's journey off! We had to think of everything a family would need: clothes, bedding, books, a few pieces of furniture, tools for building, money for paying for any help, kerosene for light, and medicines, for it took about two months to get an answer from the nearest doctor. All these things had to be put into boxes for pack-mules to carry.

And as we stood on that mountain-top looking away to the blue, mountain-lined horizon, we thought how difficult it was going to be for the animals; and, indeed, although they had started with us that morning, they were nowhere in sight now. But they would come; we must get on our way. The mountain-top experience is grand, but it is the valley that usually brings progress. Down we must go: down, down till the muscles on the back of one's legs ache with the strain; down, down until the high, free heaven is a mere memory and the cliffs and hills hem you in and try to obliterate the knowledge that this is not all that life holds. Down, down to the bottom of the abysmal ravine, where a few Chinese are trying to make a living by the banks of the rough stream which is hurrying towards the great river.

The mules did not overtake us that night, but, as the road would be fairly level for miles ahead, we started on without anxiety concerning them.

It was not pleasant travelling. True, the path lay beside the noisy little stream, but the mountains were steep, and frequently great rocks overhung the road, huge massive things suspended dangerously over one's head, and, to make matters worse, here and there we began to come upon spots where the path was almost obliterated with landslides, showing that those rocks were indeed none too securely held in place!

All morning we travelled thus, hardly seeing any human habitation. At length by noon we came upon a sulphur spring where there were a few houses of very poor Chinese. In one of these we asked if we could buy food, but there was none to be had; only wood for a fire and a small piece of rock salt. However, we had oatmeal with us, so prepared that. In the midst of our simple lunch the hot, excited face of our young muleteer appeared in the doorway.

"Pastor! We can't come over this road! The mules can never make it over these landslides. They had a hard time on the mountain yesterday, but this is the end. We can't go on. You will have to go back! Perhaps we can find another way into this place, but we can't go in by this road."

Go back? We had already come five days' journey at considerable expense. Another way in? Yes, there was such, but oh, days' and days' journey away. We could never afford such a detour. And, besides, God had led us in, and He never leads into blind alleys. Gently, my husband reasoned with the boy and attempted to persuade him to try, but he was too angry and excited. Whatever would we do? All we possessed, except that which was on the riding mule and a blanket or so in Kathryn's chair, was in those loads. This oatmeal, just finished, was the last of our food, and we were going farther and farther away from stores or supplies.

Long years ago we had been taught a prayer to use when obstacles suddenly seem to insist that we make a curve or detour from the straight path ahead. It has become a part of our lives, and it is this: "Lord, if this be from Thee, I accept it; but if it is from Satan, I refuse it." (I found it later in John Bunyan, though worded differently: "If it be of God, let me not despise it; if it be of the devil, let me not embrace it.") We prayed it now, then lifted our heads and asked each other what we felt we should do. Both were unanimous: "Go forward and *trust*."

So John turned to the muleteer and said, "You must come on. We are not going to wait for you. If you exercise care at each landslide and carry the loads over yourselves, you can make it. But you are to *try*." We knew if the loads were their own goods, they would do this.

The boy scowled blackly and shouted, "Well, if you lose all your possessions, you cannot blame us!" then disappeared.

And so with slightly troubled, at least solemnized hearts, we went on. And the landslides *grew worse* and more frequent. But at each (and over some I could hardly keep my feet, but slid and heard the gravel coming with me), when across, I stopped and committed that particular spot to the Lord, and asked that each mule, both load and animal, would come over it safely. That was done at each slide *with the exception of one*. That particular one was the last of all, and just as I was about to pray we met some passers-by who told us that, the previous week, at that particular spot, an English Consul had lost his load of supplies while trying to get into the canyon, and had turned back and gone home! Such surprising news—that an English Consul had been in those parts—drove prayer out of my mind.

It was days after we arrived at the shanty before we got word concerning our things; then we found that all the places covered with prayer had been passed in safety. *Just this one landslide* had seen accident. A mule collided with the one ahead and it with its load had gone over the embankment. Our bottles of medicine had gone into a hole in the river and could not be recovered— the mule itself was not able to stand for two hours, they said. When we heard that the animals were arriving, we ran down the path in excitement, and there sure enough was the caravan, headed by *an unloaded mule*; when I got up to him he hung his head as if he knew he had cause to be ashamed! But I am getting ahead of my story.

After passing the landslides, that night we came on to the banks of the canyon. Will I ever forget the first evening in Lisuland? After supper we went out on the wooded slopes of the mountain- side, the pine-scented, soft little breeze brushing our foreheads, and we looked up at the silent black wall of mountain across the gorge. Up beyond its sharply silhouetted edge gleamed the stars, "the scriptures of the skies." But here and there over the dark, rough surface opposite were little fires, like golden fire-flies, only steadily shining out into the night. "Those are Lisu fires," whispered my husband, and we stood and looked with hearts stirring within us. "My sheep wandered through all mountains . . . none did search after them." "Lovest thou me? Feed my lambs." This is why He had brought us here; there were His lambs, and He yearned that they might know that He loves them and has redeemed them at great cost. We gazed and then prayed that we might give bread to this multitude.

The next day at noon we arrived at a Lisu village, and from

the roadside could see the last lap of our journey. We stood on the brow of a mountain; on our left was the long river canyon with its immense peaks piercing the blue. We were on the right bank facing up the gorge; but the "bank" is just a succession of monster mountain steps with chasmy sides; down and up the puny human dot goes in order to traverse the canyon. The hill dropped away from beneath us in one of these abysmal ravines, and curling laboriously back and forth and up on the brow of the opposite mountain was our path, like a yellow-brown thread. We had yet to drop down this steep fifteen hundred feet, climb that opposite thread before arriving at the shanty which was to be our home for the future.

The Lisu fed us royally on rice, bacon and eggs. Then we dropped; then we climbed; and when the warm sun was sinking behind the opposite hills we turned the corner and looked anxiously for "home". We had asked prayer helpers to pray for a Lisu who could speak fair Chinese (of which there are almost none in this part of the canyon) to act as our interpreter until we spoke the language. Also we had asked prayer for capable servants. As we looked up the trail a short figure was coming towards us. It proved to be Job, a Lisu evangelist who could speak and read Chinese well.

"Why, Job!" we cried out in delight. "How did you know we were arriving?"

"I did not know," was the quiet response. "But God told me to come out. Where are your loads and coolies?"

"We do not know where our loads are, but the coolies carrying our cupboards must be away down the mountainside; we have not seen them since noon."

"I had better go and search for them, then. Have you a lantern? It would not do for them to get lost on this mountain in the dark." So, taking our lantern, he left us to pursue our path around the mountain curve and he himself was soon lost to our sight as he dropped down the trail.

Cheered at finding someone who could understand us, we went on, the December night setting in fast with a greyness that was chilling.

"There's the shanty!" said my husband at length, and right

before us was a small group of huts, one of which was our future home. The steep mountainside had been cut into and then levelled out; on this flat space some sapling trunks had been set upright and to them bamboo mats were tied—those were the walls. Another mat, set on top of the earth, was the floor; and big crude mats were laid over the top for a roof and held down by logs and rocks.

As we stepped inside we were chilled with the cold bleakness. The house was almost empty, save for a few rough home-made box cupboards, and dust lay everywhere. Our three-year-old girlie took one look and then said, "Mamma, *o-men to hsieh liang tien chiu tseo la, gu?*" (We'll just stay two days and then go, eh?) As she ran outside, my husband muttered something and followed her. I had a feeling that he did not want me to see his face. Left alone in the desolation, cold, no food, our loads perhaps lost, bitter cold wind blowing through the walls almost as easily as if they were of wire-netting, a lump arose in my throat and my eyes grew hot and wet. But before the tears fell I noticed a little white paper, dust-covered, on the wall, bearing a text crayoned by a Chefoo schoolboy: "My God shall supply *all* your need!" It was like a Voice, like a Presence, and it flamed out into that chill dusk like letters of fire, and all the miserable little shanty was filled with warm comfort. Why had I forgotten? I was ashamed. ... "Forgive me, Lord!" I cried in my heart and then turned and went out.

Beneath me was another hut. On entering it, I found a fire, a Lisu supper cooking, and three dear Christian Lisu who had come to be our servants were busy preparing food. My husband and Kathryn, already cosily squatting down beside the warm glow, called me to join them. The crisis was passed; from that moment on Lisuland began to make us welcome.

Small Daughter soon found a playmate and much interest in the rocks and shrub pines, over which she could climb at random. In about two days word reached us that our animals were coming, and we joyfully ran down the trail to meet them, the unloaded mule leading the caravan, as I have previously described. What a tale and flow of words these Chinese muleteers produced! Such a country. It was a wonder anybody got over such roads alive. More than once they thought they wouldn't! But what nice people the Lisu were! "Why they wouldn't take any money for our meal last night!" said they. Then one of them added something which I thought was wonderful, for he was (and still is, as far as I know) a heathen: "One night after getting through an impossible day, as we were seated around the camp-fire discussing how we ever made it, I said to the other fellows, 'Do you know, I have a feeling that Si-Mu is praying for us,'" meaning the missionary. Someone has said that God never wastes anything, and surely He was striving with those men, trying to reveal Himself to them. I do not think we ever passed through their town without someone referring to that journey, although it is the most obdurate little town in refusing the Gospel we have met.

But we were soon busy with thoughts of Christmas, which would be so shortly upon us. That is the big time of the year, when the Lisu Christians gather from all parts of the field to the place where the missionary has his home (usually), and that particular village has much work to do, as they play the part of hosts. Booths of tree boughs were built for the guests to sleep under, primitive stoves made for the cooking, a welcome arch set up, and so on.

There was rejoicing the day before Christmas, as the different villagers arrived. Someone was posted to be on the look-out, and as a single file was discerned coming over one of the trails, the look-out boy fired his gun. "Bang! Bang!" it reverberated among the rocks. We all ran out to greet the newcomers, and the Reception Committee lined up under the arch and sang the welcome song; after which the long file passed under the arch and came up to shake hands. Each guest was laden; besides his contribution toward the Christmas food, he carried a gun—or at least he carried a cross-bow and arrows—and a long knife which may serve for defence or for paring potatoes! These long knives are used for everything—cutting up a squash, butchering a pig or felling a tree.

Evening came, and, tired out, I went to bed. At my side was the house wall—remember, it was only matting—and on the other side a Lisu guest, unable to find an empty booth, decided the shelter of our house-eaves was sufficient and so made his bed there. As he leant his head comfortably against the "wall", my head, just on the other side, could not have been ten inches away. He was full of Christmas joy, and late into the night he was still lustily singing—all the louder because a few yards away a group were singing a different tune, and his voice must out-carol them or be drowned!

Christmas night they again serenaded me. This time I had an additional neighbour. At my head was another bamboo-mat partition, and on the other side Job was catechizing those who had applied for baptism. Between right-hand-neighbour's blasts of joy came the murmur of Job's voice, then an answering murmur in timid feminine accents. "It must be a girl; poor thing —she sounds nervous. Job is strict. They don't all get through by any means. Lord, help her. Oh, dear! It must be nearly mid-night. Still singing—catechizing—talking—or am I dreaming?" and the crystal stars shone down and smiled as I sank into slumber.

Noon of the day after Christmas saw a long procession filing over the mountain crest which curved to the right of the shanty. This was the baptismal group and their friends, for Christmas is a good time to examine and baptize candidates, when so many are present. The pool was a banked-up mountain stream on a very steep hillside. On the one hand stood a long line of deacons, and behind them an impromptu choir, singing, "O Happy Day." On the other side were the thinly clad line of believers waiting to go down into the water.

I spied a big jutting rock some fifty feet above, and clambered up to it, where I truly had a gallery view of all the proceedings and of the magnificent background of curving mountain-tops, sweeping sides, and the green river curling its way at the foot. Towering above all, Pine Mountain threw its shadow and blocked the sun. That rude, sturdy little mountain wind took advantage of this to mercilessly thrust teasing chilly fingers through even the warmest garment, and made one shiver.

It was a real ordeal for those baptized; a plunge into December's icy mountain water, and then to run the gauntlet of that long line of deacons, shaking hands with each, and for some a third of a mile run to reach a shelter where they might don dry clothing! Who could fail to love the dauntless spirit of these who thus made public confession of their new Master! I thought of this same ceremony at home—the carefully warmed water, the sheltered, decorated tank, a blue calsomined ceiling, also a dressing-room close at hand—and I felt how precious to their Lord these brave mountain children must be. And I thanked Him in my heart for the privilege of coming to them.

Then I saw a sweet sight. Halfway down the deacon line was a little man, quite unconscious that anyone was watching him, shaking hands with his right, and with his left hand carefully brushing off the drops of water and patting their cheeks! They came in quick succession, twenty-nine of them, so he was quite busy—a handshake, a brush, a loving pat to each. Isn't that the picture of a worthy deacon? How many extend the "right hand of fellowship" *and at the same time* the left hand of brotherly love and helpfulness to the new babes in Christ?

Christmas night I was asked to give the message (Job interpreting), and a portion of Scripture which had been with me through our recent trip became my theme: "And when they had opened their treasures, they presented unto him gifts; *gold, frankincense and myrrh*"; gold representing our wealth and our possessions, which we may offer to our King, frankincense as a type of our worship—but the myrrh? That bitter thing? Surely that can only have one meaning . . . the things we are willing to suffer for His sake. This Christmastide we are all bringing our *gold* to Him, and some are also bringing a bit of frankincense, but is anyone bringing Him *myrrh*? As I put my question, one face in the audience stood out sharply, a lean, brown face with understanding eyes that burned with hot tears. He was one who had been beaten by the feudal lord because he had become a Christian —beaten so that he could not walk for three days. Yes, in that far-away rim of the earth, in that barren mountain fastness, among those poor and ragged tribespeople, there were offerings of myrrh that Christmas Day. "Lord, I bring Thee my myrrh." That was the silent heart-cry that had taken the hurt and fear out of our journey to Lisuland. I had seldom before been able to offer Him that gift, and I have never forgotten the joy of it. Ragland knew that joy. In a message to Cambridge students, he said this: "I had almost said. 'Be ambitious to suffer'."

Isn't one cause of the coldness of our Church to-day the fact that we only offer Him "gold"? We have for a long time ceased to offer Him "myrrh". How I praise Him that He deliberately (for a little while) stripped me of human comforts, that He might teach me there is a much more thrilling joy than natural pleasures can ever give. Lisuland is a place of physical hardness and spiritual luxury, but if you have ever tasted that luxury all else will be tame for ever after.

Years afterward in the home-land, we were invited to a house, a house beautifully and perfectly furnished with all that modern art and convenience can offer. The two who owned it had no children; they worked each day to earn money to add to the house's beauty, so they were not able to live in it except at night-time and holidays. As we were shown through its perfectly ordered, spotlessly clean rooms, and I thought that two human lives were being spent just in order to maintain these things, I had a desolating sense of barrenness sweep over me. What a terrible waste! Two lives spent just for this. And then I thought of my life. I thought of the flocks of dear, warm-hearted people that run to meet us, that shout with joy at the sight of "their missionary"; that catch your hand and and pat and love it; that cry "Thank you!" with shining eyes of gratitude after a message that has fed their hearts; that pray for us every day, whether they see or hear news of us or not; of lives that are beautiful in their unconscious selflessness, made so by the power of His Cross. I thought of the times when they gathered around us and sang hymns to His praise until the room was filled with melody. And I felt what an aching tragedy those two barren human lives were —all their God-given sympathies, energizing love and passion spent on *things*. Physical hardship and spiritual luxury; physical comfort and spiritual death. Oh! that we would awaken to the real values of life!

But praise God, there are still those who know the joy of offering to Him "myrrh". After giving a missionary address at home, one sees the gifts of "gold" coming up to the front, and one wonders with a longing heart, "Won't there be any myrrh?" Most myrrh is not dramatic. There are those who would be willing to be "beaten for Christ's sake", or willing to climb over

c

landslides, but yet would be unwilling to spend a half-hour daily in prayer for His cause and His kingdom. It is *myrrh* when you say quietly to a pressing friend, "No, I cannot go for a motor ride to-night, I have something I must do," and then you spend that time in intercession for His children in some part of the world, or in some other unnoticed work for His cause. I know one who has turned down such opportunities regularly, that she may spend her evenings in mimeographing prayer news of the Lisu work, free of charge. She works all day in an office. That is "myrrh", but only the inner circle know how much she has meant, in her quiet room at home, to the work on the foreign field; and it is a continual joy to watch how her Lord sees to it that she *has* times of recreation and pleasure; she goes to places and meets people in a way that is most interesting.

And there was a retired school teacher of San Francisco, who decided to become an "intercessory foreign missionary". She took all the new China Inland Mission workers of one year, seventeen in number, as her own special responsibility and immediately began to put all the heart interest and thoughtfulness into it that a worldly person would put into making money. She wrote to each of her seventeen twice a year, and we, for one couple, delighted in answering her. She carefully marked down all data about her seventeen; their fields, the local Christians, their requests for prayer. I remember she took up our request for good house-helpers in Lisuland, and God gave us Homay and Aristarchus—never have we had such good ones since. Dear "Aunt Carrie" (as she signed herself) had special books in which she kept this data, together with photographs of her seventeen and any of their field she could get. She knew more about us and our problems than some of our own parents. And many were the blessings in the work which we could attribute directly to her prayers. When God took her Home we felt she left a gap which has never really been filled. The cost of such "myrrh" is monotony and obscurity, but again He to whom the myrrh is offered sees to it that the offerer is well repaid; though it is never given for pay, otherwise it would not be "myrrh".

"Lord, I bring Thee my myrrh."

CHAPTER FOUR

"SO LOVED THAT HE GAVE"

THE measure of our love is the measure of our gifts. I remember smiling at a young man who had just become engaged to a girl friend of mine. He turned to me one morning and said, "Do you know I love her so much I get jealous if anyone else gives her anything to make her happy! I want all her happiness to come from me." Such words may sound selfish; but that intense desire to *give* is the test sign of love.

One of the wonders of a missionary's life is to read John iii. 16, and then to *look* at the creatures for whom God gave His Beloved. "For God so loved the world that he gave his only begotten Son that whosoever believeth in him should not perish, but have everlasting life." "The world" includes everybody. In polished Western lands, where man's inward corruption is carefully covered by dainty clothes and charming manners, it is not hard to believe that God loves everyone; but when you come to heathendom, it is a different matter.

The Lisu tribespeople have lived for centuries in rickety shanties on the precipitous sides of a canyon which penetrates far into central Asia. The heathen Lisu is utterly ignorant, very degraded, his only pleasure sensuality and debauchery. He is uncouth—there is no word for "please" in all his language; and the surface of him is just as repulsive as his coarse mind. Some of the heathen Lisu are said to bathe but twice in their life, when they are born and after they are dead! Their clothing is filled with vermin and is worn until it wears off. Running sores on legs and body often add to the horror of their appearance. Yet each is a man, a human soul, and Christ said that God loves him—that Lisu whom the Chinese contemptuously call "an earth person", beside whose unkempt, dirty figure the wild animal of the forest looks decent.

And so the missionary marvels. Why does God—how *can* God

—love such a creature? Because God is hungry for man's fellow-ship and love. Jesus said the Father seeketh those who will worship Him in spirit and in truth; and in every man, in this wild Lisu, there is the capacity to be born again into God's own image through faith in the atonement of Jesus Christ, God's Son. I would like to show you what God gains for Himself when He seeks and saves one of these "earth people".

One of the first of the Lisu tribe to accept Christ as his Saviour was a stalwart farmer, who was given the name of Yo-han. He was not alone in accepting Christ; and soon a young church was growing up in the Stockade Hill district, under the leadership of a wise and courageous young missionary.[1] The infant church was taught from the first that *love gives*; the church must build its own place of worship, learn to govern itself without the white man's aid, and must pass on the word of reconciliation. Young men were urged to leave their farms and work for definite periods, and go forth to evangelize the heathen members of their own race, and of course, to go without thought of salary. "Freely ye have received, freely give." And they did it!

Year after year Yo-han watched the other fellows go out to reap in Christ's harvest, and later return with glowing reports of village after village turning to Christ, and his heart burned within him. He, too, wanted to "give", but he was married and into their family came girl after girl, but never a son! And until were was another man to take over the responsibility of the farm, Yo-han could not go very far from home. Some of the fellows were volunteering for six months and some for a year of evangelistic work. A year for Christ! Taking no pay, only perhaps enough to buy one suit of clothes when the old one wore out, and trusting to the people among whom he laboured for daily bread and shelter—that was Yo-han's ideal. But year after year such a thought had to be put out of his mind. Home duties called, and duty was always a serious matter with Yo-han.

In his village and district he began to come more and more into prominence. Fidelity to the voice of God always exalts, and in time Yo-han was made deacon. I once got a glimpse of him as the Spirit was moulding him during these years, from a Bible

[1] J. O. Fraser.

class illustration he used later on. He was hunting for an example and pulled this one out of his past life. Quite oblivious of the white listener, he told this story:

"It is necessary to keep clean! Once in the early days of my Christian life, I had a quarrel with my wife." (Grins on the part of the audience. As in all primitive lands, the stronger animal rules; Lisu heathen wives are beaten and kept under. They are not companions, they are utilities. Quarrels are frequent, especially if the wife has not produced a child, or if wine has flowed freely, and all the village are entertained by the fight. No one dreams of trying to keep it in the family.) "I was ploughing new land where the weeds were plentiful, and got angry and spoke sharply to my wife in such a way that she felt insulted and turned and ran away off to her own home. Immediately I felt stricken and went out on the mountainside and prayed. As I prayed the Holy Spirit told me to go after her and ask for forgiveness." Alert attention now! Whoever heard of a Lisu man apologizing to a woman! Just imagine thinking of such a thing! Yo-han went on: "So I did just that—went into the house, took her hand and said, 'Wife, I was wrong, please forgive me.'" It was that kind of living and teaching which made Yo-han so valuable to the Lisu church.

The six little daughters were followed at long last by the coveted small son, and Yo-han happily bought himself a Chinese Bible, Old and New Testaments. "For," said he, "I shall have my son taught to read Chinese and then he can read it to me, and I shall be able to have all the Word of God at my disposal!" So the precious book was purchased and laid up on a shelf; Yo-han could speak Chinese, but could not read it; and the Lisu had only the four Gospels and the Book of Acts translated then.[1]

So years passed, and then the eldest daughter got married and brought her bridegroom, "Elijah", into her father's house to live. With an able-bodied son-in-law to work their farm, Yo-han saw the dream of his days coming to him, and made known his intentions of giving *a year* to the Lord's work in pioneer fields. And this is when Yo-han came into our life.

Ten days' journey up the great canyon which is Lisuland, a new Lisu church was called into being in a district known as Oak

[1] The translation of the whole Bible into Lisu was completed in 1962.

Flat. The farther up the canyon, which takes its rise in Tibet, the more primitive are the people; the higher and more rugged the mountains, the greater is their need of Bible exposition; and it was to them that "Teacher" Yo-han proffered his ripe Christian experience.

We had just been in the canyon about two months when word came to us: "Five volunteer teachers from Stockade Hill have just arrived!" Soon we were entering the bamboo hut where the guests were entertained. Four picturesquely attired young men were squatting around the fire; but in their centre was one who immediately drew attention. Forty-nine years of age, neatly and simply dressed, with quiet dignity in his bearing, but with a kind, fatherly smile that made his face radiant, Yo-han inspired confidence from the first glance. "Fifteen years have I known Yo-han," wrote Mr. Fraser to us, "and in all that time I have not heard anything of him that was not in his favour!" Not a bad testimony for an earth person, is it? Do you wonder why God loves and seeks such as he? How glad we were to have him! We had not yet learned Lisu, and few of them knew Chinese. Here was one who not only could interpret for us, and teach us Lisu, but was also himself capable of feeding the flock in their own tongue, so that no time at all need be wasted until we learnt the language.

One early memory was the sight of him in church the first Sunday. "Church?" A simple building; mother earth for its carpet, braided bamboo mats for its walls, rough-hewn shelters laid on thin beams and held in place by logs or big stones; tree-trunks cut in two for benches; at night, piles of pine chips for candelabra, which throw weird shadows and gleams of light on the dark-skinned audience. But then such primitive buildings have their advantages. When the roof leaks in our grand buildings at home, what a fuss and expense of masons and plumbers! I saw the church roof leaking in Lisuland. The member of the congregation who was most discommoded merely stood on top of his bench, reached with a stick to the thatch above, wriggled it closer together and sat down in comfort—the roof was mended!

On this particular Sunday, what struck me was the contrast between speaker and audience. Yo-han had been a Christian for some fifteen years, but those before him had only come out of heathenism some few years. They had learned to wash their faces, but still had much to learn in the way of tidiness; tousled heads and garments were everywhere, whereas Yo-han was the picture of neatness, and in addition there was that uprightness of bearing which bespoke sterling character. One spot of brightness in his costume was a new book-bag his loving wife had made for him before he started on his journey. When the people become Christians, they make for themselves satchels to hold their hymn-books, catechisms and Gospel portions, and the book-bag is a matter of pride to them. But in that district little is known of embroidery; the bags are rather plain navy blue. Yo-han's bag was a thing of beauty; envelope-shaped, the flap was solid embroidery, and from the bottom edge hung rich tassels of crimson. As Yo-han stood up to speak, he noticed the eyes riveted on that delightful bag, so he paused a moment and then said, "Why have I come this long journey to visit you? Not just to see you. No, but because I have something precious to communicate to you. Now, when I start preaching I want all of you to stop looking at *me*." And he swung his beautiful bag out of sight behind his back. "Look now, if you like; but when I begin to speak, I want you to *listen to my words*!" And he pointed significantly to his lips and ears. They got the point and he held his audience!

Because of our little daughter, it was found advisable not to travel as a family, but take turns, one of us staying at home with her. The day came when I was to go with Teacher Yo-han to a nearby village, but the morning of our departure dawned grey and drizzly. Yo-han appeared at our door, his blue trousers rolled high, bare feet thrust into straw sandals, all prepared for mud and wet, but on his face was a grave expression. "Ma-ma" (my Lisu title), "it is raining and snowing to-day. You had better stay at home, for the trail will be dangerous."

"But *you* aren't staying at home, Yo-han?"

"O no!" with a glance of grave surprise that I should think such a thing.

"Well, then, I don't stay at home either!" and, disregarding his non-approval, I prepared to depart. When we were on the

path—it climbed high over rocks, dwindling to a mere foothold
—it rained, hailed and snowed so that in some places I had to
crawl on hands and feet. Then I inquired of Yo-han, "What
special danger is there when it rains that you feared for me to
come to-day?"

"When it is damp," he answered, "the great rocks above us are
apt to get loosened in the soil; then perhaps a stray animal kick-
ing with his foot causes one to come tumbling down the mountainside. You may hear it tearing through the trees above you,
but the undergrowth is so thick you cannot see it in time to get
out of the way; many of our people have been killed in this
fashion, and others mangled and hurt." So he would have had
the missionary stay at home, but would never have thought of
doing so himself!

At length, after a good hour's climb, we sighted the little
village. One wonders that houses can cling to such a declivity!
From a distance they look simply stuck on to the face of the rock;
but as you come up to them you see that the hinder part of the
hut rests on the earth, and the front part is built out over piles
or stilts, so as to make the house even. This under-the-floor space
is their animal pen, to secure their goats and oxen from thieves
and wild animals. However, once in their black windowless
insides, the foreigner becomes very much aware of the stable
underneath; through the wide cracks in the floor boards the
moving creatures can be seen—and smelt! I was amusingly
scared once, from the pit. I was seated opposite my hostess when
something that looked like a piece of raw meat down beside her
foot wriggled and was obviously alive. My hair nearly rising on
end (one hears very real things of the embodiment of evil spirits
among these animistic peoples), I leaned forward to get a better
view, and behold, it was but the tongue of a cow, stuck up
through the crack and licking a grease spot on the floor!

Once inside their shanty, I and my companion felt like resting,
while our hostess bustled around to get us something to eat. But
not so Teacher Yo-han. He had his Gospel portion out and began to study quietly. For fifteen years he had never had more
than four Gospels and the Acts, a catechism and small, much-
abbreviated book of Old Testament stories, yet he was not

tired of poring over them. It was wonderful to those of us who had heard him teach, how much he could get out of a passage! This time he had some questions to ask the young missionary.

"Ma-ma, some of our young fellow teachers, when asked by the people what this or that verse means, do not like to acknowledge their ignorance, so they make up an answer! For instance, one of them was asked what that verse means, 'Where the carcase is, there will the eagles be gathered together,' and he answered: 'It means that wherever the women are, there the men will be sure to come.' Now that wasn't correct, was it, Ma-ma? What does that verse really mean?"

Another memory of Yo-han was at a different village, this time on a Short Term Bible School trip. It was Sunday and the chapel was crowded, even some sitting on the mountainside beyond the door, peeping through to try to hear. Yo-han was to preach. As he got up to face that congregation, just out of heathenism two or three years, Yo-han got stage-fright for the only time we ever knew him to do so. Turning to us, he said, "The Word of God tells us to feed His sheep. Well, look at all those hungry faces! Oh, have I enough, this noon, to feed them?"

Yo-han was just an earth person, but he loved his Lord so much that he carried the burden of "the sheep" on his heart perpetually. "So loved that he gave." Dear, much-gifted child of modern civilization, have you ever been exercised over your Lord's other sheep? "Simon . . . *Lovest thou me? Feed* my sheep!"

A day came when a new challenge was brought to Teacher Yo-han. Six days' journey farther up the canyon another new and large Lisu church was forming. It had been suggested to Yo-han that he take a trip there and do some Bible teaching. But he smiled and answered, "Not this time. There is much more work to be done here. Perhaps I can come again and take in the Luda district."

But things were happening at Luda. A political uprising of the heathen Lisu took place simultaneously with the withdrawal of the missionaries for quite a different but urgent reason. Thus with political troubles, fighting, etc., going on, all the Christian staff had had to come away and leave those babes in Christ without a counsellor or shepherd. Sickness among ourselves prevented our going, and none of our Lisu teachers was free to go. The challenge came to Teacher Yo-han. Would he go to Luda? He did not want to go. I do not quite know why. The mountain-climbing to get there would be fatiguing in the extreme, mountains such as Yo-han's country did not know, and already he had given nearly eight months to strenuous travelling in our district. Moreover, we usually send out teachers two by two, especially on such long journeys; in case one gets sick he has a companion to attend to him. But this time there was no one who was free to go with Yo-han—only a little man to act as guide, and he a stranger to Yo-han. "So loved that he gave." Would Yo-han give up his own desires, do the thing he absolutely did not want to do, because of those "hungry sheep"; or, to be honest with ourselves, do any of us really care much about the sheep, the unknown sheep? It is the Shepherd we know and love. And, finally, for His sake, Yo-han said, "I'll go."

It was said without a smile, for it cost deeply. One of Yo-han's dearest qualities to us was his love of fun. His chuckle could lift a fellow through many a hard spot, it was so infectious, and his smile never seemed to fail. Only this time there was no smile. It was sheer determination to resist the things that pulled so strongly to keep him with us, and to "set his face" and go. So he went.

The first day out, a long day—it takes me usually two days to make that distance—Yo-han slept at the home of Christians who loved him dearly. The next morning broke rainy and wet. Lovingly, his farmer host spoke to Yo-han, "Don't go to-day, Teacher! No one knows you are coming to Luda. You aren't expected. There's no hurry! And we all know how dangerous the roads are in wet weather, not to speak of being disagreeable. Stay another day and perhaps the rain will be over!"

"Are *you* staying at home to-day?" queried Yo-han.

"Oh, no. We're in the midst of getting in our crop; we must work, but you don't have to."

"Hm! Well, I've got a crop to get in too—a crop more important than yours, my friend. I'm going on to-day." And out into the cold and wet he proceeded, with his little guide in front of him.

Details of what happened next are few. Getting near to Luda, he heard that the rope bridge across the river had been cut by the rebels, and, discouraged, he turned back. But weariness, damp and chill had done their work. Yo-han became sick in a strange, heathen home. Word reached a Christian village farther on, and some of them came down and took the helpless sick one on their backs and carried him up to their village. But all they could do— they knew so little—was unavailing. There among strangers, beloved Yo-han gave up his last gift for his Master, the same which that Master had given up for him—his life.

When news at last reached his family, his little wife was grief-stricken that she would never in this life again greet her dear husband; but after she had had time to think it all over, she made a reply that was worthy of such a man's mate. With deep emotion, she said, "It is all right; and when my son is grown I will give him too!"

"God so loved that he gave . . . and he shall see of the travail of his soul, and be satisfied."

CHAPTER FIVE

"A BURNING AND A SHINING LIGHT"

"HE was a burning and a shining light"—that was spoken of John the Baptist who said, "He must increase, but I must decrease." It is not pleasant to have to "decrease", but we cannot burn or shine without decreasing. There can be no light unless something is spent. It *costs* to shine.

I saw this in parable once. In Lisuland, sunset was the dearest time of all. For then I used to glide out of the shanty, around the hill and down on to a slim, wooded ridge which banks the river, about two thousand feet above it. As all Nature settled down to rest with vesper twitterings and a "sound of soft stilling", I liked to be quiet too, and wait in His presence while my day slipped by and folded into the irrevocable past. That ridge is sacred with memories, and one of them is a wonderful tree that used to stand there. "Parable Pine" I called him.

Tall and splendid among his fellows he stood, but when we first saw him I almost caught my breath and cried out, "Oh what a shame!" for the magnificent trunk of him had been hacked nearly half-way through by Lisu knifes. Straight, and scenting the air, he stood, but from the huge wound at his heart the sap oozed forth and dropped in long, slow tears. And then it seemed as if Parable Pine, with princely grace, stooped to my ignorant pity and spoke.

"Do you weep, friend, for my hurt and lacerated trunk? Turn and cast your eyes on that footpath high up behind you! See how it skirts the steep mountainside; look where it meets with that jutting grey rock which is too unyielding for primitive pick-axes. The trail almost disappears, becomes a mere foothold, as you go around that crag. You know how you hold your breath when you have to cross it at midday. But what if you had to go over there at night, without a light? Lisu cannot afford lanterns, you know; all they have are pine chips to light their way home. Think well, if one of your beloved Lisu were on that perilous path at a dark hour, how would he find his way over safely *without my heart*?"

And then I was taught, as in a flash, that for human souls, groping their way in the dark over dangerous paths of sin and grief, Christ needs a human heart, burning out for Him, to light their stumbling steps homeward—and who dare label it "waste"?

> Lord, in the darkness I wander,
>   Where is the lamp? Is there no lamp?
> Nothing know I, but I wonder,
>   Is there no lamp? Where is the lamp?
> Lord, in the vastness I wander,
>   Where is the way? Is there no way?
> How may I reach Thee, I wonder,
>   Is there no way? Where is the way?

In a young man's Bible were found these words: "Wanted: wicks to burn out for Christ. Oil and light furnished free." I want now to show you a Lisu wick, one who was as generous as the pine on his own mountainsides.

On the precipitous slopes of an abysmal ravine, far into Lisu-land, is a hamlet called Dried Fungus. To that hamlet came Lisu evangelists one day, and told the story of Christ's redeeming love. One whole family named Tea turned to God. But after the Christian teachers had left they were attacked by sickness, and frightened that this was the punishment of offended demons, they all renounced Christ and went back into heathenism. There was no "lamp" at that time to show them the way. All went back except one son, who had been given the name of Joseph. Joseph was really born again, and though only about twenty years of age, he refused absolutely to go back to demon worship. "All right," said his angry father. "Out you go. You can't live with us and continue to worship God."

So out the lad went on to the great mountainside, where wild beasts are and death lurks behind many a shrub and jutting rock. Rejected of his own like his Master before him, the boy turned with a heavy heart to the descending trail, slipped down the mountainside, crossed the stream at the bottom, and climbed the opposite ascent, probably little knowing what to do. However, as he went on he found a deserted hut beneath a great rock like a cave, and went in and made that his home. There he lived alone for months. But one day he fell ill, and with no one to care for him became quite sick. His father heard of it and came to his door with a pig, saying, "Son, if you will let me offer this pig in sacrifice to the demons, you will get better and you may come back home." But Joseph, sick as he was, refused.

"My Heavenly Father loves me, and I am not afraid to die. I have trusted God in health and am willing to trust Him in death." And his father had to take the pig home. But after that victory of faith Joseph got better, and one day had the joy of leading his family back to Christ.

About this time he wrote the following letter to Mr. and Mrs. Allyn Cooke. Listen to this lad not long out of heathenism:

"My dear Brother and Sister who have compassion on us,—May God give me strength and wisdom enough to remember your love even as long as God's grace exists. Big Brother and Sister, I have not words to thank you enough for bringing us the Message of Love. From the creation of the world even until now, we have never heard anything so precious. Now the news of God's love and compassion has reached our generation, and those who worship God in spirit and in truth need not enter into judgment, but are sure of a place for ever at God's right hand. Therefore I thank God and you who have taught us. Big Brother and Sister, you love us more than a father or mother, and I thank you very much.

"The writer is Joseph."

When we met this dear boy he was about twenty-five years old, of good height and proportions, and with a face that was attractive because of his sunny smile and beautiful large dark eyes which sparkled with fun one moment and glowed with loving affection the next. He was very affectionate. We always used to laugh because he found it so hard to say goodbye. He would come and shake hands with the Lisu "*Hwa-hwa*" and we thought he had gone. But no, in a few minutes here he was again, with outstretched palm wanting to say it all over again. Then we would watch him go round the corner and think, "Well now he has really gone," when lo! he appears again. "I just want to shake hands once more, Ma-pa!" Then finally he would tear himself off.

I have three Rembrandt pictures of Joseph in my memory— Rembrandt because they were all at night, and all in the chapel, where the pine chips are the only light, and as these flare up or down they sometimes throw one face into clear illumination while all the rest are in shadow.

The first picture is just to show you the boy side of him. The rough-hewn benches in chapel are divided, with men on one side and women on the other. This particular evening I happened to glance over at the men's side and the light was falling on Joseph's face but he was *not* paying attention to the sermon! He had pulled his turban down over his forehead, and his soft dark eyes were cast at the women's side of the aisle, and very obviously Joseph was sending someone an *ocular valentine*. Much amused, I turned to trace his tender glances, wondering who was the lucky recipient. And sure enough, there was a nut-brown maiden sitting with downcast eyes and trying her hardest not to look self-conscious. Ambitious Joseph! That little lady was the most desired in the district. In fact the superintendent got to hear of her many proposals and he humorously suggested (not to her of course) that she had better get refusals printed so as to save her time and embarrassment!

Picture number two is again in the shadow-flecked chapel. But this time Joseph is the preacher. He was telling the story of Daniel in the lions' den, and it became so real to him that his dark eyes dilated with fear, and his audience were sitting breathless on the edge of their benches, awaiting the awful moment when Daniel was to be demolished. Then as he answers the king's call, "O king, my God hath sent his angel and hath shut the lions' mouths," there was a general sigh of relief all over the building, and the listeners settled back to enjoy the rest comfortably. Joseph could preach.

But it was not just to exercise his gift that made him neglect his farm and go out evangelizing the heathen Lisu. His tender heart was awakened to that cry.

Where is the lamp? Is there no lamp?

. . . . .

Where is the way? Is there no way?

And Joseph left all he possessed to go and tell them that there is a Way, and to be their lamp. He became very poor materially by doing so, yet he had faith enough in little Heart's Desire to write and ask her to join him in this life of sacrifice and service. The third picture comes before he received her answer, for she said "Yes."

It was Christmas, 1935, our last before furlough, and the long chapel was packed that night as we held a testimony meeting. It was a wonderfully blessed hour, for many desired to give their testimony. Two or three were on their feet at the same moment to bear witness to what the Gospel of Christ had done in their lives, the power of His Cross and His Resurrection. Joseph was sitting well at the back, but near the centre, where the flickering glow fell full on his countenance. He was to leave very shortly for a six months' ministry in Burma. He would be seven days' journey away and would receive no salary, only his food and perhaps a bit for clothes, etc. His face was alight as he listened to the others, and again and again he made as if to rise, then checked himself to give the younger ones in Christ a chance. At length he could restrain himself no longer, and jumping to his feet he said, "How I thank God and the missionaries—Lisu and white—for bringing me this message of salvation! I haven't anything to give; but all that I am and all that I have, I give back to God!" A few days later he and the little party of Lisu Christians that had come to ask for a teacher set their faces toward that great and mighty range which on the other side is called "the Burma mountain wall".

God, in His mysterious providence, literally accepted the lad's offering that night, for at the end of his fruitful six months' service, on his way back home full of the joy of what lay before him and his marriage, Joseph was drowned in a mountain stream.[1]

When the news reached the nearest missionary, Heart's Desire happened to be present. She was tenderly told that Joseph would never now stand at the wedding altar with her, and then the brave little sweetheart slipped away to be alone. After some time, the anxious missionary heard a sound of gentle singing from the empty hut where she had gone to face her sorrow. Listening eagerly, this is what the missionary heard:

> Have Thine own way, Lord, have Thine own way.

Joseph would have wanted it so.

"And the rains of disappointment descended, and the floods of sorrow came, and the winds of questioning blew, and beat upon that house and it fell not; for it was founded upon a rock." And that Rock is Christ. Friend, is Christ the foundation of your life?

[1] It is in Burma that the Lisu church is flourishing today, and where the translation of the complete Bible into that language was completed. From Burma, too, have come Lisu Christians sometimes to witness with O.M.F. missionaries who are now living among heathen Lisu in North Thailand where, under the leadership of John and Isobel Kuhn, tribal work was started in 1952.